30 Irish Folk Songs

with sheet music and fingering for

Tin Whistle

Stephen Ducke

To download the audio files for this book, see
http://ifs1.tradschool.com

Arrangements by Stephen Ducke
Web www.tradschool.com
Email info@tradschool.com

Contents

The Good Ship Kangaroo

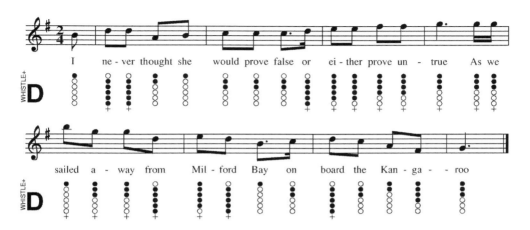

I ne-ver thought she would prove false or ei-ther prove un - true As we

sailed a - way from Mil - ford Bay on board the Kan - ga - - roo

Once I was a waiting man who lived at home at ease
Now I am a mariner that ploughs the stormy seas
I always loved seafaring life I bid my love adieu
I shipped as steward and cook me boys on board the kangaroo

I never thought she would prove false or either prove untrue
As we sailed away from Milford Bay on board the Kangaroo

Think of me oh think of me she mournfully did say
When you are in a foreign land and I am far away
And take this lucky thrupenny bit it will make you bear in mind
This loving trusting faithful heart you left in tears behind

Cheer up, cheer up my own true love don't weep so bitterly
She sobbed she sighed she choked she cried till she could not say goodbye
I won't be gone for very long but for a month or two
And when I return again of course I'll visit you

Our ship it was homeward bound from many's the foreign shore
Many's the foreign present unto my love I bore
I brought tortoises from Tenerife and ties from Timbuktu
A China rat, a Bengal cat and a Bombay cockatoo

Paid off I sought her dwelling on a street above the town
Where an ancient dame upon the line was hanging out her gown
Where is my love? she's vanished sir about six months ago
With a smart young man who drives the van for Chaplin Son & Co.

Here's a health to dreams of married life to soap suds and blue
Heart's true love, patent starch and washing soda too
Ill go into some foreign shore no longer can I stay
With some China Hottentot I'll throw my life away

My love she was no foolish girl her age it was two score
My love she was no spinster she'd been married twice before
I cannot say it was her wealth that stole my heart away

Arthur McBride

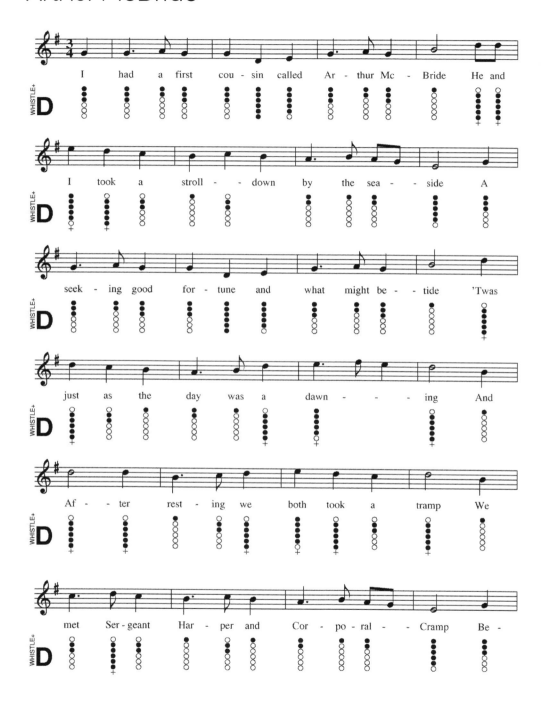

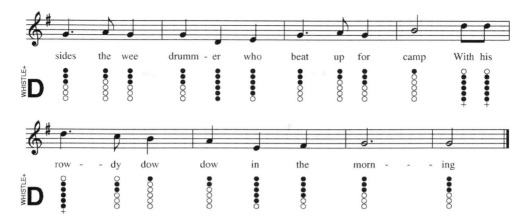

I had a first cousin called Arthur McBride
He and I took a stroll down by the by the sea side
A seeking good fortune and what might be tide
'Twas just as the day was a dawning
After resting we both took a tramp
We met Sergeant Harper and Corporal Cramp
Besides the wee drummer who beat up for camp
With his rowdy dow dow in the morning

Says he me young fellows if you will enlist
A guinea you quickly have in your fist
Likewise the crown for to kick the dust
And drink the king's health in the morning
From a soldier he leads a very fine life
He always is blessed with a charming young wife
And he pays all his debts without sorrow or strife
And always lives happy and charming

Ah now me bold sergeant we are not for sale
We'll make no such bargain, your bribe won't avail
We're not tried of our country we don't care to sail
Although that your offer is charming
And if we were such fools as to take the advance
This right bloody slander would be our poor chance
For the Queen wouldn't scruple to send us to France
Where we would be shot with out warning

He says me young fellows if I hear but one word
I instantly now will out with my sword
And into your body as strength will afford
So now my gay devils take warning
But Arthur and I we took in the odds
We gave them no chance for to launch out their swords
Our whacking shillelaghs came over their heads
And paid them right smart in the morning

As for the wee drummer we rifled his pouch
And we made a foot- ball of his rowdy dow dow
And into the ocean to rock and to roll
And bade it a tedious returning
As for the old rapier that hung by his side
We flung it as far as we could in tide
To devil I pitch you said Arthur McBride
To temper your steel in the morning

Botany Bay

Farewell to your bricks and mortar, farewell to your dirty lies
Farewell to your gangers and gang planks
And to hell with your overtime
For the good ship Ragamuffin, she's lying at the quay
For to take oul Pat with a shovel on his back
To the shores of Botany Bay

I'm on my way down to the quay, where the ship at anchor lays
To command a gang of navvys, that they told me to engage
I thought I'd drop in for a drink before I went away
For to take a trip on an emigrant ship to the shores of Botany Bay,
To the shores of botany bay

The boss came up this morning, he says "Well, Pat you know
If you don't get your navvys out, I'm afraid you'll have to go"
So I asked him for my wages and demanded all my pay
For I told him straight, I'm going to emigrate to the shores of Botany Bay

And when I reach Australia I'll go and look for gold
There's plenty there for the digging of, or so I have been told
Or else I'll go back to my trade and a hundred bricks I'll lay
Because I live for an eight hour shift on the shores of Botany Bay,

www.tradschool.com

The Harp that Once

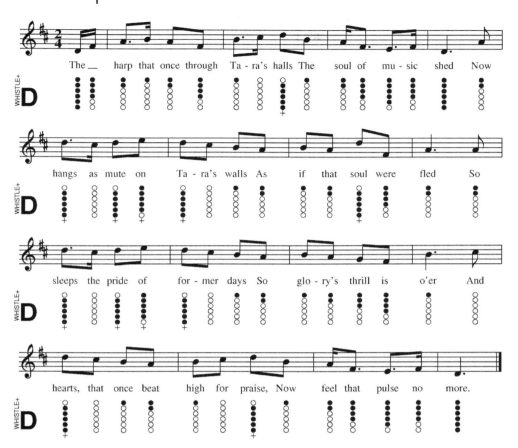

The harp that once through Tara's halls
The soul of music shed,
Now hangs as mute on Tara's walls,
As if that soul were fled. --
So sleeps the pride of former days,
So glory's thrill is o'er,
And hearts, that once beat high for praise,
Now feel that pulse no more.

No more to chiefs and ladies bright
The harp of Tara swells;
The chord alone, that breaks at night,
Its tale of ruin tells.
Thus Freedom now so seldom wakes,
The only throb she gives,
Is when some heart indignant breaks,
To show that still she lives.

Follow Me Up to Carlow

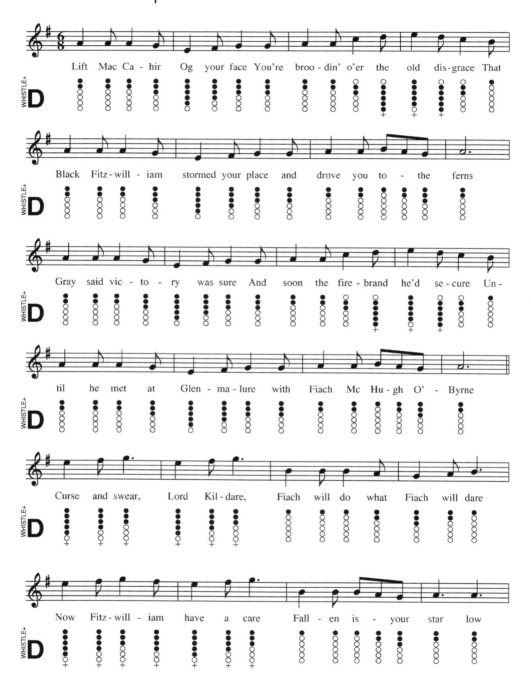

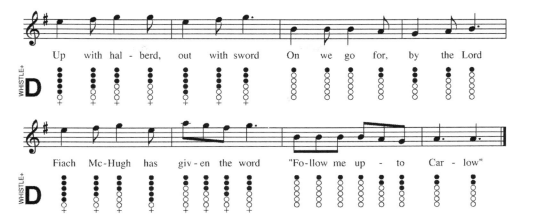

Up with hal-berd, out with sword On we go for, by the Lord

Fiach Mc-Hugh has giv-en the word "Fo-llow me up - to Car - low"

Lift Mac Cahir Og your face,
You're brooding o'er the old disgrace
That Black Fitzwilliam stormed your place
and drove you to the ferns
Gray said victory was sure,
And soon the firebrand he'd secure
Until he met at Glenmalure
with Fiach McHugh O'Byrne

Curse and swear, Lord Kildare,
Fiach will do what Fiach will dare
Now Fitzwilliam have a care,
Fallen is your star low
Up with halberd, out with sword,
on we go for, by the Lord
Fiach McHugh has given the word
"Follow me up to Carlow"

See the swords of Glen Imaal,
They're flashing o'er the English Pale
See all the childer of the Gael,
Beneath O'Byrne's banner
Rooster of the fighting stock,
Would you let a Saxon cock
Crow out upon an Irish Rock,
Fly up and teach him manners

From Tassagart to Clonmore,
There flows a stream of Saxon gore
And great is Rory Og O'More
At sending loons to Hades
White is sick and Gray is fled,
And now for black Fitzwilliam's head
We'll send it over, dripping red
to Liza and her ladies

The Wild Rover

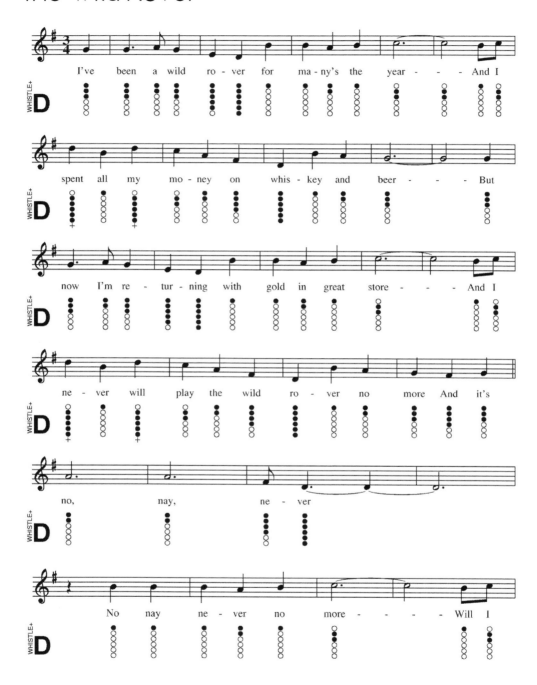

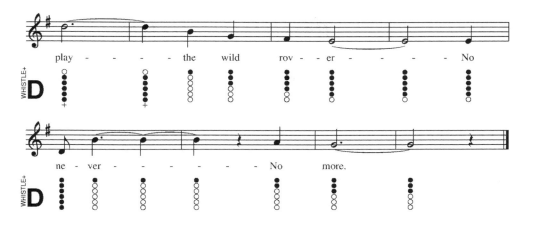

play - - - - the wild rov - - er - - - - No

ne - ver - - - - - - No more.

I've been a wild rover for many's the year
I've spent all me money on whiskey and beer
But now I'm returning with gold in great store
And I never will play the wild rover no more

And it's no, nay, never,
No, nay never no more
Will I play the wild rover,
No never no more

I went in to an alehouse I used to frequent
And I told the landlady me money was spent
I asked her for credit, she answered me nay
Such a customer as you I can have any day

I took up from my pocket, ten sovereigns bright
And the landlady's eyes opened wide with delight
She says "I have whiskeys and wines of the best
And the words that you told me were only in jest"

I'll go home to my parents, confess what I've done
And I'll ask them to pardon their prodigal son
And, when they've caressed me as oft times before
I never will play the wild rover no more

Boolavogue

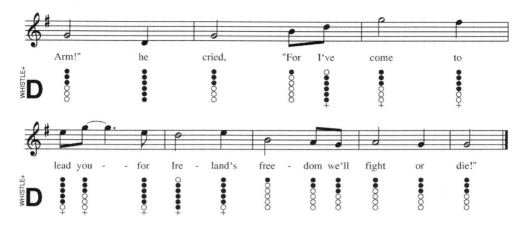

At Boolavogue as the sun was setting,
O'er the bright may meadows of Shelmalier,
A rebel hand set the heather blazing,
and brought the neighbours from far and near;

Then Father Murphy from old Kilcormack
Spurred up the rock with a warning cry:
"Arm! Arm!" he cried, "For I've come to lead you,
for Ireland`s freedom we'll fight or die!"

He lead us on against the coming soldiers,
And the cowardly Yeomen we put to flight,
'Twas at the Harrow the boys of Wexford
Showed Bookey`s regiment how men could fight;

Look out for hirelings, King George of England,
Search every kingdom where breathes a slave,
For Father Murphy of County Wexford,
Sweeps o'er the land like a mighty wave.

We took Camolin and Enniscorthy,
And Wexford storming drove out our foes,
'Twas at Slieve Coilte our pikes were reeking
With the crimson blood of the beaten Yeos.

At Tubberneering and Ballyellis,
Full many a Hessian lay in his gore,
Ah! Father Murphy had aid come over,
The Green Flag floated from shore to shore!

At Vinegar Hill o`er the pleasant Slaney,
Our heroes vainly stood back to back,
and the Yeos at Tullow took Father Murphy,
and burnt his body upon a rack.

God grant you glory, brave Father Murphy,
And open Heaven to all your men,
the cause that called you may call tomorrow,
in another fight for the Green again.

The Rare Old Mountain Dew

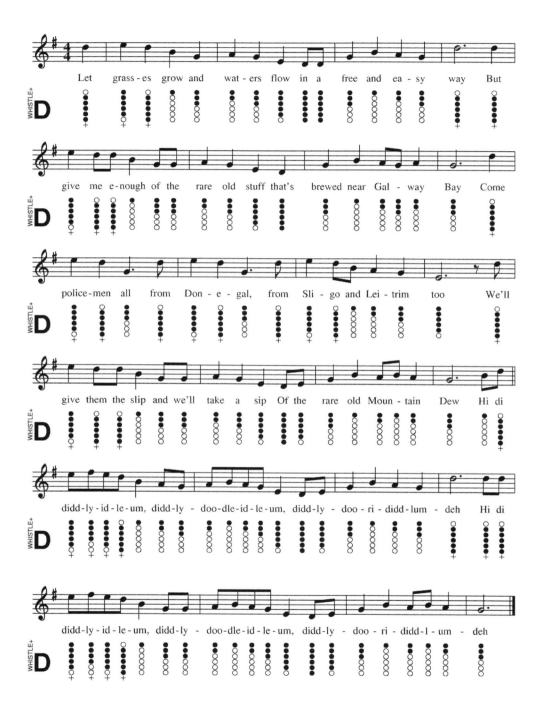

Let grasses and waters flow in a free and easy way,
But give me enough of the rare old stuff that's brewed near Galway Bay,
Come policemen all from Donegal, Sligo and Leitrim too,
Oh, we'll give them the slip and we'll take a sip
Of the rare old Mountain Dew

Hi di-diddly-idle-um, diddly-doodle-idle-um, diddly-doo-ri-diddlum-deh
Hi di-diddly-idle-um, diddly-doodle-idle-um, diddly-doo-ri-diddlum-deh

At the foot of the hill there's a neat little still,
Where the smoke curls up to the sky,
By the smoke and the smell you can plainly tell
That there's poitin brewing nearby.
For it fills the air with a perfume rare,
And betwixt both me and you,
As home we troll, we can take a bowl,
Or a bucket of the Mountain Dew

Now learned men who use the pen,
Have sung the praises high
Of the rare poitin from Ireland green,
Distilled from wheat and rye.
Put away with your pills, it'll cure all ills,
Be ye Pagan, Christian or Jew,
So take off your coat and grease your throat
With a bucket of the Mountain Dew.

The Boys of Fairhill

The smell on Patrick's Bridge is wicked
How does Father Matthew stick it?
Here's up them all says the boys of Fairhill

The Blarney hens don't lay at all
And when they lay they lay 'em small
Here's up them all says the boys of Fairhill

The Blackpool girls are very rude
They go swimming in the nude
Here's up them all says the boys of Fairhill

Blackpool boys are very nice
I have tried them once or twice
Here's up them all says the boys of Fairhill

If you come to Cork you'll get drisheen
Murphy's stout and pigs crubeens
Here's up them all says the boys of Fairhill

Well, Christy Ring he hooked the ball
We hooked him up, balls and all
Here's up them all says the boys of Fairhill

The Cliffs of Dooneen

You may travel far far from your own native home
Far away across the mountains far away o'er the foam
But of all the fine places that I've ever seen,
There's none to compare with The Cliffs of Dooneen

Take a view o'er the water fine sights you'll see there
You'll see the high rocky slopes on the West coast of Clare
The towns of Kilrush and Kilkee can be seen
From the high rocky slopes at The Cliffs of Dooneen

Its a nice place to be on a fine Summer's day
Watching all the wild flowers that ne'er do decay
The hare and lofty pheasant are plain to be seen
Making homes for their young round The Cliffs of Dooneen

Fare thee well to Dooneen fare thee well for a while
And to all the fine people I'm leaving behind
To the streams and the meadows where late I have been
And the high rocky slopes of The Cliffs of Dooneen

The Well Below the Valley

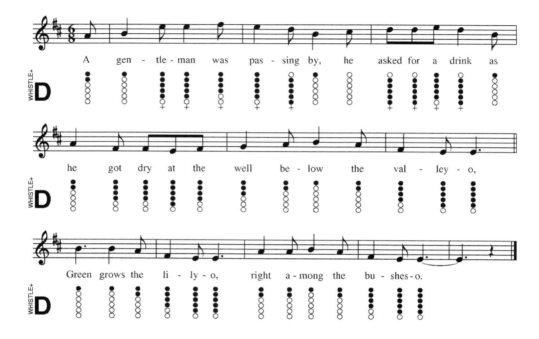

Green grows the lily-o
Right among the bushes-o

A gentleman was passing by
And he asked for a drink as he was dry
At the well below the valley-o
Green grows the lily-o
Right among the bushes-o

My cup is full up to the brim
And if I were to stoop I might fall in
At the well below the valley-o
Green grows the lily-o
Right among the bushes-o

If your true love was passing by
You'd fill him a drink if he was dry
At the well below the valley-o
Green grows the lily-o
Right among the bushes-o

She swore by grass, she swore by corn
Her true love had never been born
At the well below the valley-o
Green grows the lily-o
Right among the bushes-o

He said to her you're swearing wrong
Six fine children you've had born
At the well below the valley-o
Green grows the lily-o
Right among the bushes-o

If you be a man of noble fame
You'll tell to me the father of them
At the well below the valley-o
Green grows the lily-o
Right among the bushes-o

There's one of them by your brother John
At the well below the valley-o
One of them by your Uncle Don
At the well below the valley-o
Two of them by your father dear
At the well below the valley-o
Green grows the lily-o
Right among the bushes-o

If you be a man of noble fame
You'll tell to me what did happen to them
At the well below the valley-o
Green grows the lily-o
Right among the bushes-o

There's one of them buried beneath the tree
At the well below the valley-o
Another two buried beneath the stone
At the well below the valley-o
Two of them outside the graveyard wall
At the well below the valley-o
Green grows the lily-o
Right among the bushes-o

If you be a man of noble fame
You'll tell to me what will happen myself
At the well below the valley-o
Green grows the lily-o
Right among the bushes-o

You'll be seven years a-ringing a bell
At the well below the valley-o
And seven years a-burning in hell
At the well below the valley-o

I'll be seven years a-ringing a bell
But the Lord above may save my soul
From burning in hell at the well below the valley-o
Green grows the lily-o
Right among the bushes-o
Green grows the lily-o
Right among the bushes-o

Do You Love an Apple

Do you love an apple, do you love a pear? Do you love a laddie with curly brown hair? And still, I love him — I can't deny him I'll be with him where ev - er he goes

Do you love an apple, do you love a pear?
Do you love a laddie with curly brown hair?
And still, I love him, I can't deny him
I'll be with him where ever he goes

Before I got married I wore a black shawl
But now that I'm married I wear bugger-all
And still I love him…

He stood at the corner, a fag in his mouth
Two hands in his pockets, he whistled me out
And still I love him…

He works at the pier, for nine pound a week,
Saturday night he comes rolling home drunk
And still I love him…

Before I got married I'd sport and I'd play
But now, the cradle gets in me way
And still I love him…

Do you love an apple, do you love a pear?
Do you love a laddie with curly brown hair?
And still, I love him, I can't deny him
I'll be with him where ever he goes

The Waxie's Dargle

Says my auld one to your auld one
Will you come to the Waxie's dargle
Says your auld one to my auld one
Sure I haven't got a farthing
I've just been down to Monto town
To see Uncle McArdle
But he wouldn't lend me a half a crown
To go to the Waxie's dargle

What'll you have, will you have a pint
Yes, I'll have a pint with you, sir
And if one of us doesn't order soon
We'll be thrown out of the boozer

Says my auld one to your auld one
Will you come to the Galway races
Says your auld one to my auld one
With the price of my auld lad's braces
I went down to Capel Street
To the pawn shop money lenders
But they wouldn't give me a couple of bob
On my auld lad's red suspenders

Says my auld one to your auld one
We've got no beef nor mutton
But if we go down to Monto town
We might get a drink for nothing
Here's a piece of good advice
I got from an auld fish-monger
When food is scarce and you see the hearse
You'll know you've died of hunger

The Galway Races

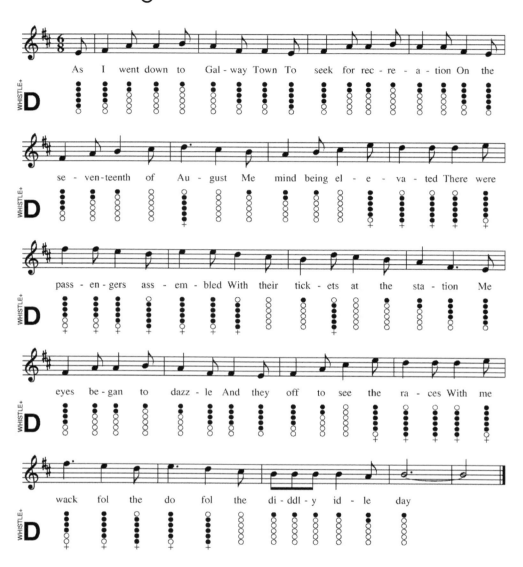

As I went down to Galway Town
To seek for recreation
On the seventeenth of August
Me mind being elevated
There were passengers assembled
With their tickets at the station
And me eyes began to dazzle
And they off to see the races

With me wack fol the do fol
The diddle idle day

There were passengers from Limerick
And passengers from Nenagh
The boys of Connemara
And the Clare unmarried maiden
There were people from Cork City
Who were loyal, true and faithful
Who brought home the Fenian prisoners
From dying in foreign nations

And it's there you'll see the pipers
And the fiddlers competing
And the sporting wheel of fortune
And the four and twenty quarters
And there's others without scruple
Pelting wattles at poor Maggie
And her father well contented
And he gazing at his daughter

And it's there you'll see the jockeys
And they mounted on so stably
The pink, the blue, the orange, and green
The colours of our nation
The time it came for starting
All the horses seemed impatient
Their feet they hardly touched the ground
The speed was so amazing!

There was half a million people there
Of all denominations
The Catholic, the Protestant, the Jew, the Presbyterian
Yet there was no animosity
No matter what persuasion
But failte hospitality
Inducing fresh acquaintance

Johnny I Hardly Know Ye

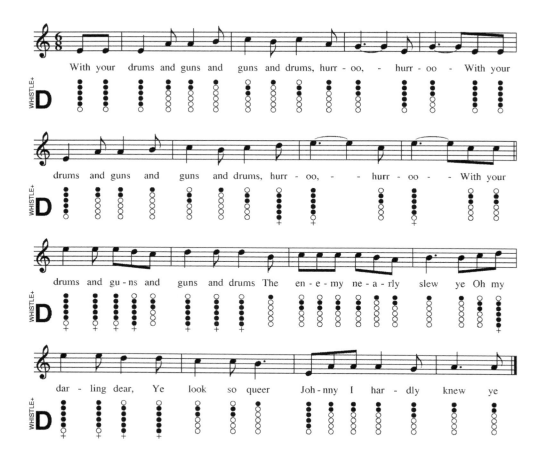

While going the road to sweet Athy, hurroo, hurroo
While going the road to sweet Athy, hurroo, hurroo
While going the road to sweet Athy
A stick in me hand and a tear in me eye
A doleful damsel I heard cry,
Johnny I hardly knew ye.

With your drums and guns and guns and drums, hurroo, hurroo
With your drums and guns and guns and drums, hurroo, hurroo
With your drums and guns and guns and drums
The enemy nearly slew ye
Oh my darling dear, Ye look so queer
Johnny I hardly knew ye.

Where are the eyes that looked so mild, hurroo,
hurroo
Where are the eyes that looked so mild, hurroo,
hurroo
Where are the eyes that looked so mild
When my poor heart you first beguiled
Why did ye scadaddle from me and the child
Oh Johnny, I hardly knew ye.

Where are your legs that used to run, hurroo,
hurroo
Where are your legs that used to run, hurroo,
hurroo
Where are your legs that used to run
When you went to carry a gun
Indeed your dancing days are done
Oh Johnny, I hardly knew ye.

I'm happy for to see ye home, hurroo, hurroo
I'm happy for to see ye home, hurroo, hurroo
I'm happy for to see ye home
All from the island of Ceylon
So low in the flesh, so high in the bone
Oh Johnny I hardly knew ye.

Ye haven't an arm, ye haven't a leg, hurroo,
hurroo
Ye haven't an arm, ye haven't a leg, hurroo,
hurroo
Ye haven't an arm, ye haven't a leg
Ye're an armless, boneless, chickenless egg
Ye'll have to be put with a bowl out to beg
Oh Johnny I hardly knew ye.

They're rolling out the guns again, hurroo,
hurroo
They're rolling out the guns again, hurroo,
hurroo
They're rolling out the guns again
But they never will take my sons again
No they'll never take my sons again
Johnny I'm swearing to ye.

Danny Boy

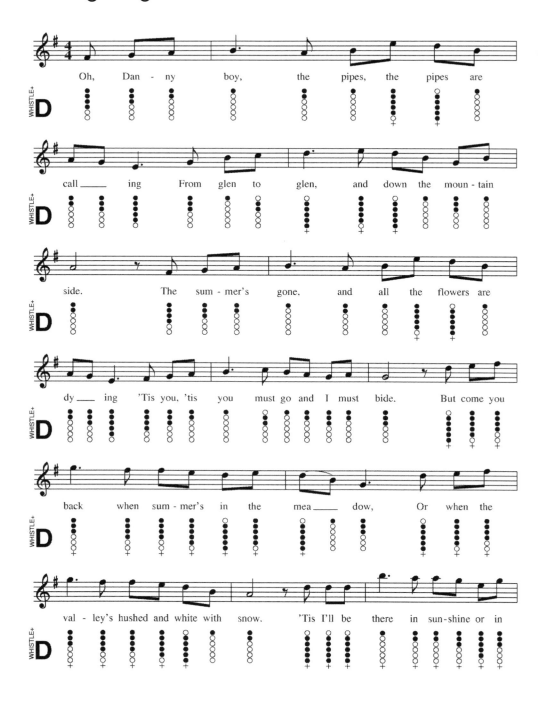

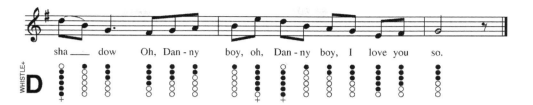

sha___dow Oh, Dan - ny boy, oh, Dan - ny boy, I love you so.

Oh Danny boy, the pipes, the pipes are calling
From glen to glen, and down the mountain side
The summer's gone, and all the flowers are dying
'Tis you, 'tis you must go and I must bide.

But come ye back when summer's in the meadow
Or when the valley's hushed and white with snow
'Tis I'll be here in sunshine or in shadow
Oh Danny boy, oh Danny boy, I love you so.

But when he come, and all the flowers are dying
If I am dead, as dead I well may be
You'll come and find the place where I am lying
And kneel and say an "Ave" there for me.

And I shall hear, tho' soft you tread above me
And all my grave will warm and sweeter be
For you will bend and tell me that you love me
And I shall sleep in peace until you come to

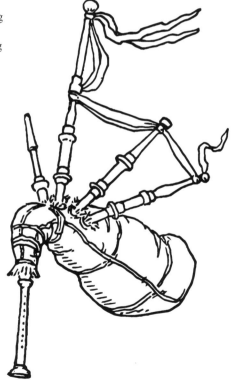

High Germany

Oh Poll-y love, oh Po-lly the rout has now be-gun A-nd we must go-a mar-ching at the beat-ing of-the drum Go-dress your-se-lf a-ll in your best and come a-long with me I-'ll take you to the war-me love in High--Ger-ma-ny

Oh Willy love, oh Willy come list to what I say
My feet they are so tender, I can not march away
And besides my dearest Willy I am with child by thee
Not fitted for the war me love in High Germany

I'll buy for you a horse me love and on it you shall ride
And all my life I'll be there riding by your side
We'll stop at every ale-house and drink when we are dry
We'll be true to one another, get married bye and bye

Oh cursed be the cruel wars that ever they should rise
And out of merry England press many a man likewise
They pressed my true love from me, likewise my brothers three
And sent them to the wars me lad in High Germany

My friends I do not value nor my foes I do not fear
Now my love has left me I wander far and near
And when my baby it is born and smiling on my knee
I'll think of lovely Willy in High Germany

I'll Tell My Ma

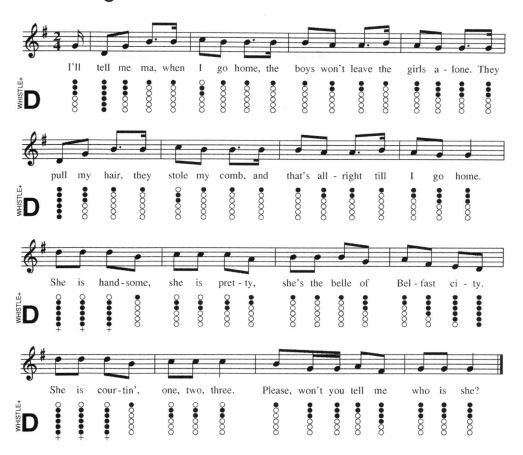

I'll tell me ma, when I go home, the boys won't leave the girls a-lone. They
pull my hair, they stole my comb, and that's all-right till I go home.
She is hand-some, she is pret-ty, she's the belle of Bel-fast ci-ty.
She is cour-tin', one, two, three. Please, won't you tell me who is she?

I'll tell me Ma when I go home
The boys won't leave the girls alone.
They pull my hair, they stole my comb,
but that's alright till I go home.

She is handsome, she is pretty
She is the belle of Belfast city
She is courting one, two, three.
Please won't you tell me, who is she?

Albert Mooney says he loves her,
All the boys are fighting for her.
They knock at the door and ring at the bell
Saying "Oh, my true love are you well?"

Out she comes as white as snow,
Rings on her fingers and bells on her toes.
Oul Jenny Murray says she'll die,
If she don't get the fellow with the roving eye.

Let the wind and the rain and the hail blow high
and the snow come tumbling from the sky
She's as nice as apple pie
And she'll get her own lad by and by.
When she gets a lad of her own,
she won't tell her Ma when she goes home
Let them all come as they will
For it's Albert Mooney she loves still.

Galway Bay

'Tis far away I am today from scenes I roamed a boy,
And long ago the hour I know I first saw Illinois;
But time nor tide nor waters wide can wean my heart away,
For ever true it flies to you, my dear old Galway Bay.

My chosen bride is by my side, her brown hair silver-grey,
Her daughter Rose as like her grows as April dawn to day.
Our only boy, his mother's joy, his father's pride and stay;
With gifts like these I'd live at ease, were I near Galway Bay.

Oh, grey and bleak, by shore and creek, the rugged rocks abound,
But sweet and green the grass between, as grows on Irish ground,
So friendship fond, all wealth beyond, and love that lives alway,
Bless each poor home beside your foam, my dear old Galway Bay.

A prouder man I'd walk the land in health and peace of mind,
If I might toil and strive and moil, nor cast one thought behind,
But what would be the world to me, its wealth and rich array,
If memory I lost of thee, my own dear Galway Bay.

Had I youth's blood and hopeful mood and heart of fire once more,
For all the gold the world might hold I'd never quit your shore,
I'd live content whate'er God sent with neighbours old and gray,
And lay my bones, 'neath churchyard stones, beside you, Galway Bay.

The blessing of a poor old man be with you night and day,
The blessing of a lonely man whose heart will soon be clay;
'Tis all the Heaven I'll ask of God upon my dying day,
My soul to soar for evermore above you, Galway Bay.

The Bantry Girl's Lament

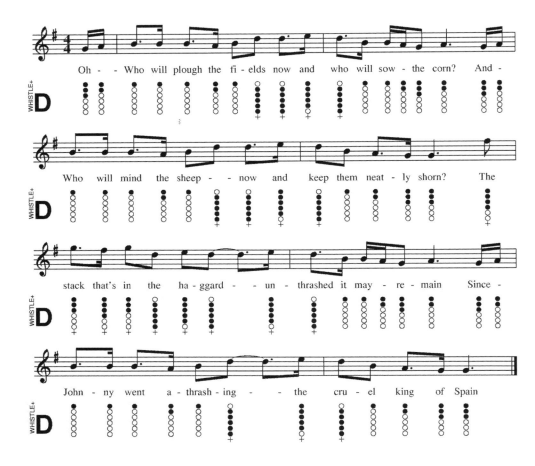

Oh, Who will plough the fields now and who will sow the corn?
Who will mind the sheep now and keep them neatly shorn?
The stack that's in the haggard, unthrashed it may remain
Since Johnny's went a-thrashing the dirty king of Spain
The girls from the bawnogue in sorrow may retire
And the piper and his bellows go home and blow the fire
Since Johnny, lovely Johnny is sailing o'er the main
Along with other patriots to fight the King of Spain

The boys will surely miss him when Moneymore comes round
And they'll find that their bold captain is nowhere to be found
And the peelers must stand idle, all against their will and main
Since the gallant boys who gave them work now peels the King of Spain

At wakes or hurling matches your like we'll never see
Till you come back to us again, *a stór grá geal mo chroí*
And won't you thrash the buckeens that show us much disdain
Because our eyes are not so bright as those you'll meet in Spain

If cruel fate will not permit our Johnny to return
His heavy loss we Bantry girls will never cease to mourn
We'll resign ourselves to our sad lot and die in grief and pain
Since Johnny died for Ireland's pride in the foreign land of Spain

Lanigan's Ball

In the town of Athy one Jeremy Lannigan battered away 'til he hadn't a pound
His father he died and made him a man again left him a farm and ten acres of ground
He gave a grand party to friends and relations who didn't forget him when come to the wall
And if you but listen I'll make your eyes glisten at rows and ructions at Lannigan's Ball

Myself to be sure, got free invitation for all the nice boys and girls that I ask
In less than a minute the friends and relations were dancing as merry as bees round a cask
There were lashing of punch and wine for the ladies Potatoes and cake, bacon and tea
There were the Nolan, Dolans, O'Grady's courting the girls and dancing away

They were doing all kinds of nonsensical polkas all around in a whirligig
Julia and I soon banished their nonsense out on the floor for a reel and jig
How the girls all got mad at me danced till they thought the ceilings would fall
I spent six months in Brooks Academy learning to dance for Lannigan's Ball

Six long months I spent in Dublin, six long months doing nothing at all
Six long months I spent in Dublin learning to dance for Lannigan's Ball
She stepped out, I stepped in again, I stepped out and she stepped in again
She stepped out, I stepped in again, learning to dance for Lannigan's Ball

The boys were merry the girls all hearty dancin' around in couples and groups
An accident happened - Terence McCarthy put his right boot through Miss Finnerty's hoops
The creature she fainted and cried, "Milia murder." Called for her brothers and gathered they all
Carmody swore he'd go no further till he got revenge at Lannigan's Ball

Boys oh boys 'tis then there was ructions I got a kick from young Phelim McHugh
I soon replied to his fine introduction kicked him a terrible hullabaloo
Casey the piper was near gettin' strangled they leapt on his pipes, bellows, chanter and all
Boys and girls all got entangled and the put an end to Lannigan's Ball

The Lark in the Morning

Oh, the lark in the morning she rises off her nest,
She goes off in the air with the dew all on her breast;
And like the jolly ploughboy she whistles and she sings,
She goes home in the evening with the dew all on her wings.

Oh, Roger the ploughboy he is a dashing blade,
He goes whistling and singing all through the leafy glade;
He nests at dark at Susan's, she's handsome, I declare,
She's far more enticing than the birds all in the air.

As they were riding home from the fair all in the town,
Well, the madder was so kissable and the heather was mowed down;
'Twas there they jumped and tumbled all in the new mown hay,
Said, "Take me now or never," this young lass she did say.

When twenty long weeks had all of them gone past,
Well, her mother asked the reason why she thickened 'round the waist;
"It was the jolly ploughboy," this young lass she did say,
"He caused me for to tumble all in the new-mown hay."

So, here's a health to the ploughboy wherever you may be,
Would you like to have a bonnie lass a-sitting on your knee;
With a pint of good strong porter she makes a lovely ring,
She'll make your farmer happier than a prince or a king.

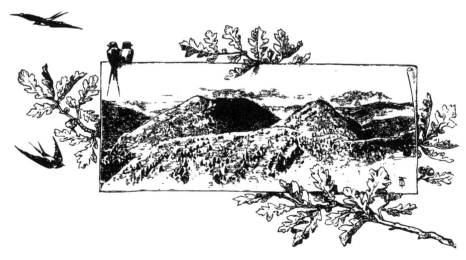

The Rising of the Moon

And come tell me Sean O'Farrell tell me why you hurry so
Hush, *a buachaill*, hush and listen and his cheeks were all a glow
I bear orders from the captain get you ready quick and soon
For the pikes must be together by the rising of the moon

By the rising of the moon, by the rising of the moon
For the pikes must be together by the rising of the moon

And come tell me Sean O'Farrell where the gathering is to be
At the old spot by the river quite well known to you and me
One more word for signal token whistle out the marching tune
With your pike upon your shoulder by the rising of the moon

Out from many a mud wall cabin eyes were watching through the night
Many a manly heart was beating for the blessed warning light
Murmurs rang along the valleys to the banshee's lonely croon
And a thousand pikes were flashing by the rising of the moon

All along that singing river that black mass of men was seen
High above their shining weapons flew their own beloved green
Death to every foe and traitor! Whistle out the marching tune
And hurrah, me boys, for freedom, 'tis the rising of the moon

'Tis the rising of the moon, 'tis the rising of the moon
And hurrah, me boys, for freedom, 'tis the rising of the moon

The Last Rose of Summer

'Tis the last rose of summer,
Left blooming alone;
All her lovely companions
Are faded and gone;
No flower of her kindred,
No rosebud is nigh,
To reflect back her blushes,
Or give sigh for sigh.

I'll not leave thee, thou lone one!
To pine on the stem;
Since the lovely are sleeping,
Go, sleep thou with them.

Thus kindly I scatter,
Thy leaves o'er the bed,
Where thy mates of the garden
Lie scentless and dead.

So soon may I follow,
When friendships decay,
And from Love's shining circle
The gems drop away.
When true hearts lie withered,
And fond ones are flown,
Oh! who would inhabit
This bleak world alone?

A Bunch of Thyme

Come all ye maidens young and fair And you that are blooming in your prime Always beware and keep your garden fair no man steal away your thyme

Come all ye maidens young and fair
And you that are blooming in your prime
Always beware and keep your garden fair
Let no man steal away your thyme

 For thyme it is a precious thing
And thyme brings all things to my mind
Thyme with all its flavours, along with all its joys
Thyme, brings all things to my mind

Once I had a bunch of thyme
I thought it never would decay
Then came a lusty sailor who chanced to pass my way
And stole my bunch of thyme away

The sailor gave to me a rose
A rose that never would decay
He gave it to me to keep me reminded
Of when he stole my thyme away

The Leaving of Liverpool

Farewell to you my own true love
I am going far away
I am bound for California
But I know that I'll return some day

So fare thee well, my own true love
And when I return, united we will be
It's not the leaving of Liverpool that grieves me
But, my darling, when I think of thee

I have sailed on a yankee sailing ship
Davy Crockett is her name
And Burgess is the captain of her
And they say she is a floating shame

I have sailed with Burgess once before
And I think I know him right well
If a man is a sailor, he can get along
But if not than he's surely in hell

Oh, the fog is on the harbour love
And I wish I could remain
But I know it will be some long time
Before I see you again

Weile Waile

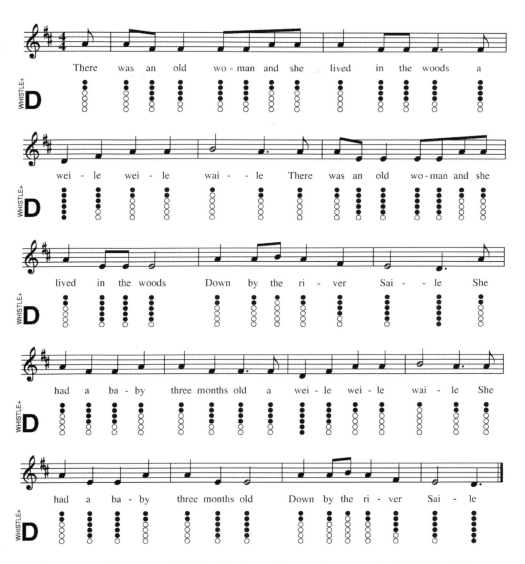

There was an old woman and she lived in the woods…

She had a penknife long and sharp…

She stuck the penknife in the baby's heart…

Three policemen came knocking on the door…

Are you the woman that killed the child …

The rope was pulled and she got hung…

And that was the end of the woman in the woods,
A weile weile waile
And that was the end of the baby too
Down by the river Saile

The Black Velvet Band

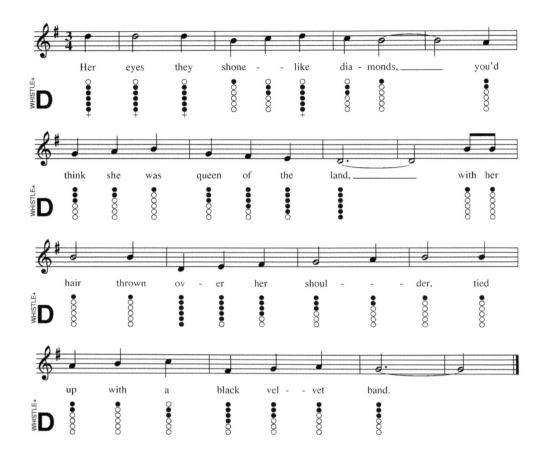

Well, in a neat little town they call Belfast, apprentice to trade I was bound
Many an hours sweet happiness, have I spent in that neat little town
A sad misfortune came over me, which caused me to stray from the land
Far away from my friends and relations, betrayed by the black velvet band

Her eyes they shone like diamonds
I thought her the queen of the land
And her hair it hung over her shoulder
Tied up with a black velvet band

I took a stroll down Broadway, meaning not long for to stay
When who should I meet but this pretty fair maid comes a tripping along the highway
She was both fair and handsome, her neck it was just like a swans
And her hair it hung over her shoulder, tied up with a black velvet band

I took a stroll with this pretty fair maid, and a gentleman passing us by
Well I knew she meant the doing of him, by the look in her roguish black eye
A gold watch she took from his pocket and placed it right in to my hand
And the very first thing that I said was bad luck to the black velvet band

Before the judge and the jury, next morning I had to appear
The judge he says to me: "Young man, your case it is proven clear
We'll give you seven years penal servitude, to be spent far away from the land
Far away from your friends and companions, betrayed by the black velvet band"

So come all you jolly young fellows a warning take by me
When you are out on the town me lads, beware of them pretty colleens
For they feed you with strong drink, until you are unable to stand
And the very next thing that you'll know is you've landed in Van Diemen's Land

Whiskey in the Jar

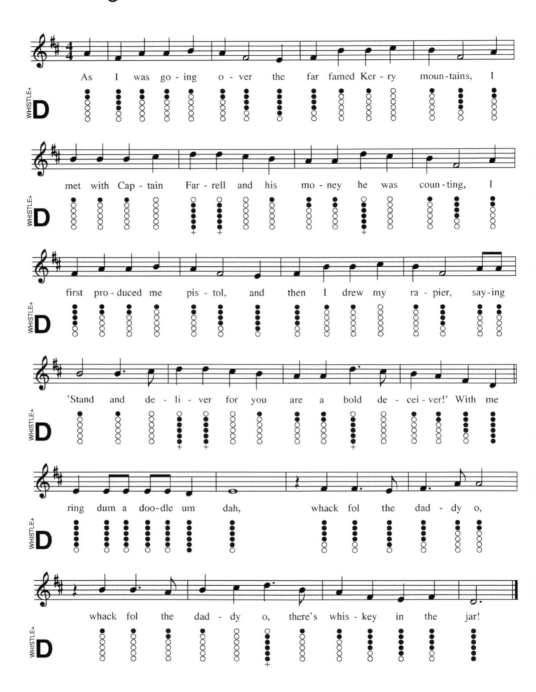

As I was a going over the far famed Kerry mountains
I met with captain Farrell and his money he was counting
I first produced my pistol and I then produced my rapier
Saying "Stand and deliver for you are a bold deceiver"

With me ring dum a doo-dle um dah,
Whack fol the dad-dy o,
Whack fol the dad-dy o,
There's whiskey in the jar

I counted out his money and it made a pretty penny
I put it in me pocket and I took it home to Jenny
She sighed and she swore that she never would deceive me
But the devil take the women for they never can be easy

I went up to my chamber, all for to take a slumber
I dreamt of gold and jewels and for sure 't was no wonder
But Jenny drew me charges and she filled them up with water
Then sent for captain Farrell to be ready for the slaughter

'Twas early in the morning, just before I rose to travel
Up comes a band of footmen and likewise captain Farrell
I first produced me pistol for she stole away me rapier
I couldn't shoot the water, so a prisoner I was taken

Now there's some take delight in the carriages a rolling
and others take delight in the hurling and the bowling
but I take delight in the juice of the barley
and courting pretty fair maids in the morning bright and early

If anyone can aid me 'tis my brother in the army
If I can find his station in Cork or in Killarney
And if he'll go with me, we'll go roving through Killkenny
And I'm sure he'll treat me better than my own a-sporting Jenny

Down by the Glenside

'Twas down by the glenside, I met an old woman
She was picking young nettles and she scarce saw me coming
I listened a while to the song she was humming
Glory O, Glory O, to the bold Fenian men

'Tis fifty long years since I saw the moon beaming
On strong manly forms and their eyes with hope gleaming
I see them again, sure, in all my daydreaming
Glory O, Glory O, to the bold Fenian men.

When I was a young girl, their marching and drilling
Awoke in the glenside sounds awesome and thrilling
They loved poor old Ireland and to die they were willing
Glory O, Glory O, to the bold Fenian men.

Some died on the glenside, some died near a stranger
And wise men have told us that their cause was a failure
They fought for old Ireland and they never feared danger
Glory O, Glory O, to the bold Fenian men

I passed on my way, God be praised that I met her
Be life long or short, sure I'll never forget her
We may have brave men, but we'll never have better
Glory O, Glory O, to the bold Fenian men

Appendix : Playing the Tin Whistle

You will find in the following pages some basic information to help you begin playing the tunes in this book on the whistle.

Holding the whistle

The whistle has 6 holes, which are covered with the first three fingers of each hand. The left hand fingers cover the top three holes, while the right hand covers the bottom (if you're left-handed, you may feel more comfortable with the right hand on top).

Grip the tip of the mouthpiece firmly between the lips (not the teeth) and rest the barrel on the thumbs; if held firmly at the mouthpiece, it shouldn't move. To make a sound, hold the whistle without covering any holes and blow a long, steady stream of air.

Tablatures & playing your first notes

In the tablatures that accompany the airs in this collection, the 6 holes of the whistle are represented by a diagram; open holes are indicated by white circles, while closed holes are black.

To play your first notes on the whistle, start with the C# (C sharp) which is played all holes open.

Then lower one finger at a time, starting with the left index (on the hole nearest the mouthpiece of the whistle) as in the diagram below:

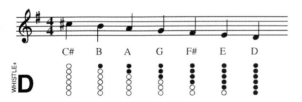

Be careful that the holes are properly covered, but without clenching the whistle too tightly - this will take some practise at the start. If a certain note doesn't play (or makes a creaking or squeaking sound) then it is probably because a hole is not properly covered and leaking air. If this happens, start at the top again and come back down.

The first octave

Here are all the notes of the first octave, starting with low D:

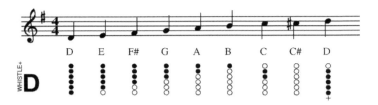

The second octave

To play the second or higher octave, the fingering doesn't change except for the high D. For all other notes, you just need to blow slightly harder. On the fingering tablatures, the second octave is indicated by the plus symbol.

For the tunes in this collection, there is no need to play higher than the high B.

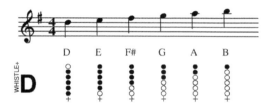

The scale of D

Here is the scale of D :

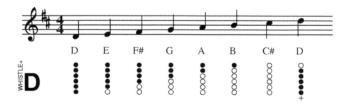

The scale of G

Here is the scale of G, with one new note, C natural.

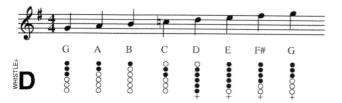

Here is the complete range of notes you will play on the tin whistle

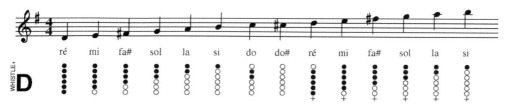

THE TUNEBOOK SERIES

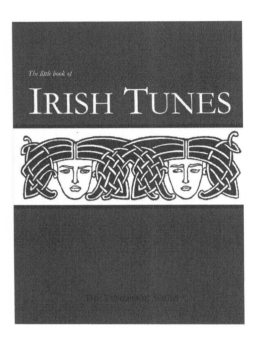

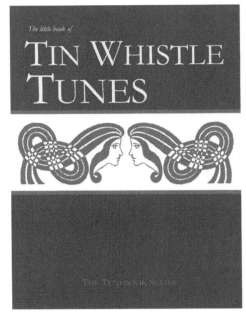

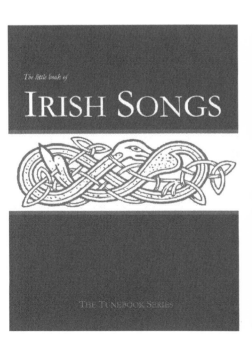

TIN WHISTLE FOR BEGINNERS

Tin Whistle for Beginners : easy Irish songs and Tunes with fingering guides for Tin Whistle

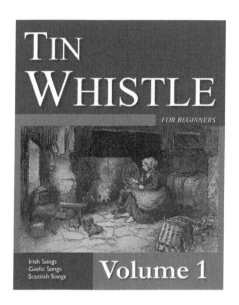

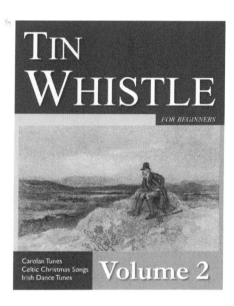

Whistle for Kids : easy tin whistle tunes for children

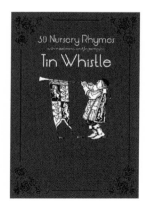

ALSO AVAILABLE

Irish Music - 400 Traditional Tunes

184 pages, with audio download

Classic Irish Session Tunes from the author of "A Complete Guide to Playing Irish Traditional Music on the Whistle". A unique collection of the most popular tunes played in Ireland ... and throughout the world. Complete with 400-track audio download of each tune played at moderate speed on Tin Whistle.

Stephen Ducke is an Irish flute and whistle player from County Roscommon. Musician for over 30 years and an inspired teacher, he has recorded one solo album and is author and editor of several books of Irish and traditional music.

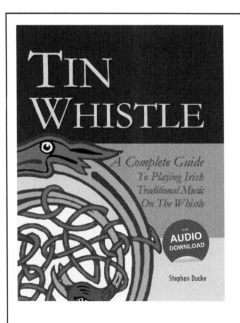

A Complete Guide to Playing Irish Traditional Music on the Whistle

286 pages; with 429 accompanying audio tracks

This tutor book, with its accompanying audio files, is intended to give a complete introduction to playing Irish music in the traditional style on the tin whistle; it covers all from the very first notes on the instruments to the most advanced ornamentation.

It is intended for anybody who wants to play traditional music in the Irish style, from complete beginners to confirmed or advanced players who wish to work on their style or ornamentation. Tablature as well as sheet music is used throughout the book, so it is accessible to the complete beginner; while more advanced players will appreciate the attention to detail in style and ornamentation in the later parts of the book.

Made in the USA
Las Vegas, NV
10 January 2021